21st Century Skills Library

LIFE SKILLS BIOGRAPHIES

ANDREW CARNEGIE

Sarah De Capua

Cherry Lake Publishing
Ann Arbor, Michigan

Published in the United States of America by Cherry Lake Publishing
Ann Arbor, MI
www.cherrylakepublishing.com

Content Adviser: Gino Francesconi, Librarian, Carnegie Hall Archives, New York, New York

Photo Credits: Cover and pages 1, 9, 14, 20, 23, 24, 28, 33, 42, and 43, Photos courtesy of the Library of Congress; pages 6, 11, 30, 34, and 40, © Bettmann/Corbis; page 13, © Corbis; page 37, © Andrew Holbrooke/Corbis; page 38, © The Scotsman/Corbis Sygma

Library of Congress Cataloging-in-Publication Data
De Capua, Sarah.
  Andrew Carnegie / by Sarah DeCapua.
    p. cm. — (Life skills biographies)
  Includes index.
  ISBN-13: 978-1-60279-067-4
  ISBN-10: 1-60279-067-1
  1. Carnegie, Andrew, 1835–1919—Juvenile literature. 2. Industrialists—United States—Biography—Juvenile literature. 3. Philanthropists—United States—Biography—Juvenile literature. I. Title. II. Series.
  CT275.C3D43 2008
  361.7'4092—dc22
  [B]   2007005861

Cherry Lake Publishing would like to acknowledge the work of
The Partnership for 21st Century Skills.
Please visit www.21stcenturyskills.org for more information.

Contents

INTRODUCTION

The 19th century was a time of rapid growth in the United States. In 1800, the country was 24 years old. The nation extended from the Atlantic Ocean in the east to the Mississippi River in the west. It included only 16 states and several large territories. The biggest cities were Philadelphia, New York, and Boston. The population of each was under 70,000. By 1900, the nation had long since celebrated its centennial, or 100th birthday. The country stretched from the Atlantic to the Pacific. Twenty-nine more states had joined the Union. Cities such as Pittsburgh, Chicago, and San Francisco were bustling with businesses, factories, and hundreds of thousands of people.

In 1800, the population of the United States was 5,308,483. Just 100 years later, the population had exploded to 76,212,168. Many of these people were the descendants of settlers who had arrived during the 1600s and 1700s. They had British, French, Spanish, German, and Dutch roots. Some were descended from Caribbean or African slaves. But other groups contributed more to the U.S. population explosion. In the 1800s, millions of immigrants, usually poor, left their native lands to begin new lives in the United States.

These immigrants contributed much to the growth and development of the United States. Many simply made better lives for their families. Others became more successful than they ever could have imagined. One who grew to be truly **prosperous** was a Scottish immigrant who became involved with the railroad, the telegraph, and the iron and steel industries. He was in the middle of many of the changes that helped shape the country in the 1800s and beyond. During a time when many men made extraordinary fortunes, his fortune was the biggest. For a time, he was the world's richest man. His name was Andrew Carnegie.

CHAPTER ONE

HUMBLE BEGINNINGS

In the 1830s, Dunfermline, Scotland, was a town of 13,000 people. Located about 15 miles (24 kilometers) northwest of Edinburgh, the country's capital, Dunfermline was near the country's plentiful coalfields. The town consisted of several factories, which were dirty and hot. Clean water was scarce. There was no plumbing or sewer system. Homes usually had only a few rooms in which large families lived together. In these conditions, diseases such as cholera and typhus were common.

Andrew Carnegie's birthplace in Dunfermline, Scotland, is now a museum.

It was in this town that Andrew Carnegie was born on a cold, gray day. The date was November 25, 1835. Andrew's father, William Carnegie, was a highly skilled weaver. He specialized in damask, a type of weaving that uses cotton, linen, or silk to create flat patterns in a shiny weave. Weaving was one of the town's major industries at the time. Andrew's mother, Margaret Carnegie, was a homemaker. Andrew—or Andra, as his family called him—was the oldest of three children. Andrew's sister, Ann, was born in 1840. She died before she was one year old. His brother, Tom, was born in 1843.

In 1843, eight-year-old Andrew began attending school. It was there that he developed what would become a lifelong interest in books and reading. As a hobby, Andrew kept pigeons and rabbits in a hutch his father had built in the backyard. In one of his first business deals, Andrew convinced his friends to spend Saturdays helping him gather dandelions and clover as food for the rabbits. In return, he promised to name newborn rabbits after each of them. This taught Andrew that people would work for him if he made them feel important.

Young Andrew enjoyed visiting his uncle, George Lauder, who was called Uncle Lauder. Uncle Lauder

As a boy, Andrew Carnegie had to walk to a well every morning before school to get a bucket of water for his mother. Some of the water she used for cleaning. She also boiled some of it to kill off impurities so the family could drink clean water. This daily chore taught Andrew the value of responsibility and discipline.

Life & Career Skills

William Wallace
(1270–1305) was a
Scottish patriot who led
a revolt against English
rule. He rallied and
motivated many of his
fellow patriots to join
in the fight. Wallace's
forces defeated the
army of England's
king Edward I
on September 11,
1297. Wallace was
later captured by
the English. He was
executed for **treason** on
August 22, 1305.

owned a small grocery store in Dunfermline. His son, George, was Andrew's cousin and best friend. The two boys enjoyed Uncle Lauder's stories of Scotland's history. Many of the kings, queens, and princes of early Scotland were born, had lived, or were buried in Dunfermline, which was once Scotland's capital. Through Uncle Lauder, Andrew became fascinated by Scottish heroes, such as William Wallace and Robert the Bruce. He read and memorized many of the works of Scottish poet Robert Burns. Andrew also learned about the United States and some of its heroes, including George Washington, Thomas Jefferson, and Benjamin Franklin.

THE POWER OF STEAM

In 1843, a steam-powered **textile** factory opened in Dunfermline. The Industrial Revolution had arrived in Scotland. During the Industrial Revolution, the economies of many countries changed rapidly because of the introduction of machine-driven factories. Factory owners hired unskilled women and children to work steam-powered looms, the machines used to weave cloth. These factories could produce cloth quickly and cheaply. Weavers who worked handlooms, such as Andrew's father, saw their businesses shrink. People didn't want to buy expensive cloth from William Carnegie—and wait weeks for him to weave it—when they could pay less for factory-made cloth produced much more quickly. The loss in business forced Carnegie to sell three of his four looms and dismiss his **apprentices**.

With William Carnegie barely able to make a living, Margaret Carnegie saved her family from total poverty by opening a small store in the front room of their cottage. She sold vegetables, flour, salt, tobacco, and candy to neighborhood families. At night, she stitched shoes for a local shoemaker.

In the summer of 1847, another large steam-powered **textile** factory opened in Dunfermline. Four hundred weavers found jobs there, but not

Andrew was inspired by Uncle Lauder's stories of Scotland's history.

William Carnegie. The following winter, Andrew's father arrived home one night after searching unsuccessfully for orders for handwoven damask. Deeply disappointed, he told his son, "Andra, I can get [no more] work."

A COUNTRY FAR BETTER

Two of Margaret Carnegie's sisters, Annie and Kitty, lived in the United States. By 1840, the women and their husbands had journeyed across the Atlantic and settled near Pittsburgh, Pennsylvania. In letters to their sister, Annie and Kitty often tried to convince Margaret to move her family to America. One letter said: "[America] is far better for the workingman than [Scotland], and there is room enough to spare, notwithstanding the thousands that flock into her borders every year. As for myself, I like it much better than [Scotland]."

After many discussions, William and Margaret realized they had little choice. William didn't have enough work to feed his family. And despite Margaret's best efforts, their money was running out. They decided that the family would leave Scotland.

In the spring of 1848, William and Margaret sold their furniture and many other belongings. They used this money and money they borrowed from a neighbor to book ship passage. Then they set off from Dunfermline for the city of Glasgow in a horse-drawn carriage. In Glasgow, they boarded the ship *Wiscasset*. Twelve-year-old Andrew and his family soon began their seven-week voyage from Scotland to the United States.

CHAPTER TWO

JOURNEY TO AMERICA

*During the 19th century, many immigrants to the
United States arrived at New York Harbor.*

On August 14, 1848, the *Wiscasset* steamed into New York Harbor. Andrew Carnegie was about to become one of the 189,176 immigrants who arrived in New York City that year. Though they had reached America, the Carnegies' journey was not yet complete. No passenger train ran between New York and Pittsburgh, so the family traveled there on small, steam-powered boats over canals, rivers, and Lake Erie. The trip to Pittsburgh took another three weeks.

The Carnegies settled in Allegheny City, a factory town of 10,000 people—mostly immigrants—located across the Allegheny River from Pittsburgh. They settled into two rooms located above a tiny loom shop behind the home of Margaret's sister Kitty and her husband, Thomas. (Andrew and Tom called them Aunt Kitty and Uncle Hogan.) William Carnegie immediately set out to find work. He borrowed a loom like the one he'd had in Dunfermline and wove fine damask table linens, which he sold door-to-door. He didn't sell many, though. Just as in Dunfermline, his handmade linens were far more expensive than linens made in factories. Again running out of money and facing hunger, the family worried that perhaps their long journey to America had been for nothing.

Margaret once more kept the family from going hungry by sewing shoes for a neighbor who was a shoemaker. At that time, the Carnegies needed $7.50 a week to feed the family, but Margaret was earning only $4.00 a week. By January 1849, William Carnegie found work at a local cotton mill. The mill owner employed young

*The Allegheny River meets the Monongahela River
in Pittsburgh to form the Ohio River.*

boys to do simple tasks. Because the family could not afford to send
Andrew or Tom to school, Andrew went to work.

Andrew was 13 years old when he began working as a bobbin boy at
the same cotton mill where his father worked. His salary was $1.20 a week.

*During the 1800s and early 1900s, it was common
for children to work in factories.*

Bobbin boys moved around the factory floor with supplies of bobbins, the cylinders around which yarn or thread is wound. The bobbin boys loaded the bobbins onto the machines' spindles, the rods or pins that held the bobbins in place. Once yarn was wound onto a bobbin, a boy removed it. It wasn't hard work, but it was boring and repetitive, and Andrew worked 12 hours a day, six days a week. Still, he saw the bright side: with his help, the family was eating well and beginning to succeed in their adopted homeland.

THE BOBBIN FACTORY

A short time after Andrew started working at the cotton mill, another factory owner offered him a job for $2.00 a week. Andrew accepted because he wanted to earn more money. He worked in the dark basement of a bobbin factory on the small steam engine that powered the factory's machinery. He shoveled woodchips into the fire in order to maintain the temperature of the boiler, the part of the engine where water is heated until it turns to steam. If the fire did not have enough woodchips, the water would not heat into steam. Without enough steam, the factory's machinery lost power. If too many woodchips were put on the fire, there was too much steam. This could cause the boiler to explode. Steam boiler explosions could cause serious injuries, such as burns from the scalding water and steam, and even death.

In his autobiography, Andrew Carnegie recalled nightmares in which he struggled to keep the boiler at the right temperature. He would awaken sitting up in bed, sweating and frightened. He didn't tell his parents of his fears and nightmares. He remembered the stories of William Wallace and other heroes, which made him feel better. And he looked forward to a day when he wouldn't have to work in the basement of the bobbin factory anymore.

One day the factory owner was struggling with paperwork. He had poor penmanship. He asked Andrew to write out the bills. Andrew was happy for the **opportunity**. It was a chance to get away from the boiler. The office work didn't take much time, however, so Andrew also worked dipping newly made wooden bobbins into vats of oil. Dipping bobbins in oil helped preserve the wood so the bobbins would last longer. Andrew hated the smell of the oil. It often made him sick. He worked alone, so he had little to take his mind off his work. Still, he remained positive, recalling, "My hopes were high, and I looked every day for some change to take place."

Andrew continued to work during the day. At night, he took a class in bookkeeping to learn how to keep track of an office's business and accounts. Fourteen-year-old Andrew was motivated by the hope that his bookkeeping skills would help him get away from the vat of oil for good.

THE TELEGRAPH OFFICE

Andrew's Uncle Hogan played checkers with a man named David Brooks. Brooks was the manager of a telegraph office in Pittsburgh. Business was good, and Brooks needed another boy to deliver telegrams. Hogan suggested that Andrew was just the right boy for the job.

When Uncle Hogan told Andrew and his parents about the job—and the salary of $2.50 a week—Andrew and his mother were excited about the opportunity. But Andrew's father worried that Andrew was too young, too inexperienced, and too small for the job of delivering telegrams around Pittsburgh. Andrew was small for his age, and even as an adult, he was only 5 feet 3 (160 centimeters), 4 inches (10 cm) shorter than the average American man at the time. But Andrew and his mother convinced his father to let Andrew try the job.

The next morning, Andrew reported to the telegraph office in the only nice clothes he had. His enthusiasm and willingness to memorize all the city's streets so he could make deliveries quickly convinced Brooks to hire him. Andrew immediately set out to deliver his first telegram.

FROM MESSENGER BOY TO TELEGRAPH OPERATOR

Andrew enjoyed delivering messages around Pittsburgh. If a message had to be delivered to a fruit store or a bakery, sometimes he was paid in fresh fruit or delicious baked goods. Deliveries to theaters

Learning & Innovation Skills

The telegraph, a system of transmitting messages over long distances, was commonly used in the latter half of the 19th century. It uses electricity to send a series of signals. Samuel F. B. Morse was an American artist and inventor who developed what came to be called Morse code. Morse code is a system of short, or dot (•), and long, or dash (—), keystrokes. These keystrokes stand for letters of the alphabet. For example, • — stands for the letter A. The dots and dashes were translated into messages called telegrams. Delivery boys took the messages from telegraph offices to the recipients.

Life & Career Skills

Colonel James Anderson was a wealthy man who lived near the Carnegies. He had a library in his home. His collection contained more than 400 books. Because Allegheny City did not have a public library, every Saturday Anderson allowed his neighbors to borrow books for one week at a time. Andrew borrowed books more often than anyone else in the community. Thankful for the opportunity, he took the initiative to educate himself. He later wrote, "Colonel Anderson opened to me the intellectual wealth of the world." For the rest of his life, Andrew Carnegie would consider libraries an **invaluable** resource.

allowed him to watch shows for free. Andrew enjoyed these extra benefits of his job.

Messages that required delivery to towns beyond Pittsburgh earned him an extra 10¢. A few months after going to work for Brooks, Andrew got a raise. Now he was earning more than $2.50 a week. He added his wages to the money his parents made. His mother was still sewing shoes, and his father, unhappy with his factory job, had returned to selling handmade linens door-to-door. Soon, the Carnegies were able to repay their neighbor in Scotland who had given them money for their ship passage to America. This was another important lesson in responsibility and honesty for Andrew and his brother.

Shortly after Andrew's family repaid the loan, Andrew's Aunt Kitty and Uncle Hogan moved to Ohio. The Carnegies rented the Hogans' two-story house. Andrew and Tom were thrilled to have a big house of their own.

Andrew arrived early at the telegraph office every morning and swept it out. This quiet time at the office gave him a chance to practice using the telegraph machine. Before long, Andrew could send and receive messages on his own.

At that time, the dots and dashes of incoming messages were marked on a piece of paper by the telegraph. A person translated them into written messages in English. But Andrew taught himself how to recognize Morse code by the tapping sounds the machine made for each letter. He was said to be only the third person in the United States with this skill. He could write out the messages as they came in, instead of waiting for someone to translate them. This saved a lot of time and allowed important messages to be delivered faster.

By the time he was 16 years old, Andrew had been promoted to telegraph operator. He got the promotion only 18 months after he had been hired as a messenger. He now earned $25 a month, an excellent salary at that time. For an additional dollar a day, he made copies of overseas news that came in over the telegraph to be sold to local newspapers. Andrew's income made it possible for the Carnegies to buy a home of their own.

CHAPTER THREE

TO THE RAILROAD AND BEYOND

Andrew Carnegie excelled in the railroad industry and was promoted to supervisor by the age of 24.

Andrew's skill at translating Morse code by sound was so unusual that people would go to the telegraph office to watch him work. Well-known businessmen noticed him. They chose him to send their important messages. One of these men was Thomas A. Scott, the superintendent of the Western Division of the Pennsylvania Railroad. Scott liked Andrew's cheerfulness, energy, and ability to do a lot of work in a short amount of time. Scott offered him a job. Andrew saw that his future might be brighter with the railroad industry instead of the telegraph industry. He jumped at the chance to advance his career. In February 1853, 17-year-old Andrew Carnegie went to work for the railroad.

At that time, most cities were connected by only one railroad track. Passenger and freight trains going in both directions had to share the track. To avoid collisions, telegraph operators sent messages from station to station so that train conductors knew when they had to move their trains off the main track and onto an extra track alongside the main track. This practice was called siding. Because telegraph operators were in charge of siding, they were important to the railroad industry. Carnegie's first job for the railroad was sending and receiving messages that helped trains travel safely between Pittsburgh and Philadelphia.

Carnegie soon learned many of Scott's responsibilities. He accompanied Scott to investigate construction progress, maintenance, and accidents. This meant a lot of traveling, even in bad weather, but Carnegie enjoyed this part of his job.

Carnegie had been working for the railroad for two years when his father died. He was deeply saddened by the loss, especially because William Carnegie never achieved the wealth he had sought in America. But Carnegie was comforted by the fact that his father had lived to see the family become financially comfortable, with a house of their own.

A year later, Scott received a promotion that required him to move to another office of the Pennsylvania Railroad. Carnegie went with him to the new office, in Altoona, Pennsylvania, about 85 miles (140 km) east of

Pittsburgh. Carnegie's mother and brother moved to Altoona with him. For the next three years, Carnegie continued to work closely with Scott, learning the railroad business.

In 1859, Scott received another promotion, to vice president of the railroad company. Carnegie was also promoted. He took over Scott's old position as superintendent of the Western Division of the Pennsylvania Railroad. The promotion increased Carnegie's salary to $125 a month, and he moved his family back to Pittsburgh. With Carnegie's promotion, the family could afford to move to an upper-class area. They settled in Homewood, a neighborhood in the town of East Liberty, a few miles from Pittsburgh. The three Carnegies moved into a small house surrounded by spruce trees. Margaret Carnegie, who no longer needed to work to help support the family, settled into a comfortable life. She enjoyed gardening and social gatherings with her Homewood neighbors. Tom Carnegie became his brother's assistant at the railroad office.

AMERICAN CIVIL WAR SERVICE

When the Civil War broke out in April 1861, both Thomas Scott and Andrew Carnegie were called to Washington, D.C., to lead work crews repairing railroad and telegraph lines that linked the nation's capital to states in the North. The Northern states, which supported the federal government, were called the Union. The railroad tracks and telegraph lines had been destroyed by people who supported the South, or the Confederacy. It was important to repair the tracks so that the Union could move its soldiers and materials easily.

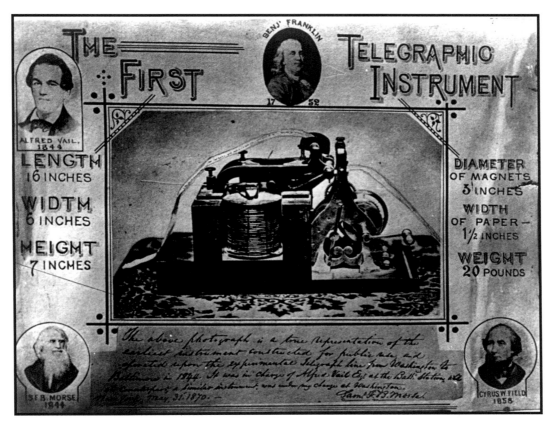

Telegraph transmission was an important means of communication during the Civil War.

With that project successfully completed, Carnegie began putting together a new telegraph service for the War Department. This new service became the 1,500-member Telegraph Corps. These telegraph operators helped President Abraham Lincoln, the War Department, and the Union army stay in communication during the war.

Carnegie left Washington in November 1861. The following summer, he and his mother went to Scotland for a long visit. They returned to

On many early sleeper cars, the upper compartments with sleeping platforms were shut during the day.

Pittsburgh in the autumn of 1862. Carnegie continued running the railroad and making every effort to help the Union army in its struggle against the Confederacy.

The war ended in April 1865 with a Union victory. A month before the war ended, Carnegie made a risky decision: he quit the Pennsylvania Railroad. As superintendent of the Western Division, Carnegie was well placed to make a fortune as the railroad expanded after the war ended. But he left his secure job to pursue a different future. He became a full-time **investor**.

SLEEPING CARS

Before the Civil War, Carnegie had invested in sleeping cars, an **innovation** in train travel. As railroad routes expanded, people took longer trips. They needed comfortable railroad cars to sleep in. Theodore Woodruff developed a sleeping car that had a hinged compartment above the seats. The compartment folded down to become a sleeping platform with a cushion on it. The Pennsylvania Railroad paid Woodruff to make four sleeping cars. This development in rail travel looked promising, so Carnegie invested in Woodruff's company. The sleeping cars became so popular that Woodruff's company could barely keep up with the orders. Soon, Carnegie was making far more money than he had invested. In the coming years, he was able to use the funds to make other investments.

ON TO OIL

In August 1859, a man named Edwin Drake struck oil in a field near Titusville, Pennsylvania, about 90 miles (145 km) north of Pittsburgh. Drake was a retired train conductor who had been hired to drill in the area. Drake was soon pumping so much oil that others began to drill nearby.

21st Century Content

Carnegie was not yet 30 years old. He had a secure job and a steady income. As a superintendent of the Pennsylvania Railroad, he had the opportunity to become wealthy as the railroad built more tracks. But he was interested in becoming an **entrepreneur**, and he decided to concentrate on being an investor. Relying on investments for income is risky. The amount of money made from investments can vary. Most people prefer the security of a steady income. But Carnegie left the railroad to pursue investments in unproven industries, such as oil and iron.

As word of the oil fields spread, Carnegie decided to see for himself what all the fuss was about. Together with his brother and a friend, Carnegie visited the site. He decided that oil use had a future in the United States. Carnegie bought a large farm near Drake's oil field and organized the Columbia Oil Company. Shortly afterward, oil was found on his farm. By 1862, the company was pumping more than 2,000 barrels of oil a day. The oil pumped from Carnegie's wells earned him nearly $18,000 in the first year alone. The profits continued for years to come.

THE PROMISE OF IRON

Until 1858, most railroad bridges were made of wood. But the wood often rotted, causing bridge collapses, or caught fire from the sparks coming out of train smokestacks. Carnegie had seen railroad bridges in England that were constructed of iron. He believed that iron railroad bridges should be built throughout the United States.

In 1858, workers constructed a small iron bridge in Altoona. Carnegie organized the men who built that bridge into a company called the Keystone Bridge Company. By 1863, the company was on its way to making strong iron bridges across all the major American rivers.

These businesses—the sleeping cars, the Columbia Oil Company, and the Keystone Bridge Company—made it possible for Carnegie to quit the railroad as the Civil War was winding down. He was making plenty of money through his own businesses. As a result, he created other companies. He founded the Superior Rail Mill, which made iron rails for railroad tracks. He also founded the Pittsburgh Locomotive Works, which made train engines. The Union Iron Mills, which produced iron for bridges, trains, railroad tracks, and sleeping cars, was another Carnegie company.

A NEW HOME

In late 1867, Carnegie and his mother moved to New York City. (Tom, who had gotten married and started a family, stayed in Homewood.) The Carnegies first lived in what was then the finest hotel in America—the St. Nicholas Hotel. Its staircases were made of marble, and crystal chandeliers hung from the ceilings. The walls were covered with gleaming mirrors and expensive artwork. Carnegie and his mother stayed in several interconnected rooms. They were amazed by how much their lives had changed since their arrival in America less than 20 years before.

In 1879, they moved to the Windsor Hotel, located on Fifth Avenue. Margaret Carnegie would live there for the rest of her life. Carnegie himself would move on to other, grander New York homes.

Carnegie's boyhood friends from Allegheny City and Homewood—and his brother, Tom—held important positions in his businesses. Part of Carnegie's success was his ability to collaborate with others. He sometimes disagreed or even argued with them over business dealings. But when business was finished, he returned to friendly terms with them. Throughout his life, Carnegie remained close to his circle of trusted friends.

CHAPTER FOUR

STEEL KING AND PHILANTHROPIST

The Edgar Thomson Steel Works, located on the Monongahela River, is still in operation today.

While iron was an important building material, Carnegie soon realized that steel was an even more promising one. In England, an engineer and inventor named Henry Bessemer found a way to blast hot air through **molten** iron to burn away the impurities. This made steel. Because it has fewer impurities, steel is stronger and, thus, is a better building material than iron. Carnegie traveled to England to see Bessemer's process in person. Afterward, he concluded that iron was no longer useful in the construction of railroads, ships, buildings, bridges, and machinery. "Steel is king," he told his business partners.

THE EDGAR THOMSON STEEL WORKS

In 1872, Carnegie returned from his trip to England determined to build a steel mill. Together with friends, business associates, and his brother, Carnegie chose a site southeast of Pittsburgh and hired a company to build the mill. Upon completion, the Edgar Thomson Steel Works was the largest and most modern steel mill in the United States. On September 1, 1875, the mill produced its first of 2,000 rails ordered by the Pennsylvania Railroad.

Tom Carnegie ran the mill's day-to-day operations. Andrew Carnegie traveled often, meeting with railroad owners and convincing them to purchase the steel his mill produced. Carnegie's instincts, natural abilities, and shrewd business sense helped him sell a lot of steel. In its first full year of operation, the mill produced 21,674 tons (19,662 metric tons) of steel. By 1878, it was making more steel than any other steelworks in the country. Carnegie truly was the king of steel.

CARNEGIE BROTHERS AND COMPANY

With the steelworks producing so much steel, Carnegie soon had more steel than was needed to fill railroad orders. He began selling the steel to Pittsburgh **buggy** makers, farmers (for their plows), and homeowners

Some consider the Home Insurance Building in Chicago, Illinois, to be the first skyscraper. It was built in 1885.

(for stovepipes and gutters). His company was efficient and well run, and Carnegie paid the men in charge high salaries, which kept them happy and loyal to the company.

In 1881, Carnegie merged, or brought together, all of his companies—including the steelworks, the Union Iron Mills, and the Keystone Bridge Company—into one big corporation. Carnegie Brothers and Company was the largest company of its kind in the United States, and Carnegie owned more than half of it. His brother and other investors owned the rest.

In late 1883, Carnegie purchased a rival steel mill called the Homestead Works. This mill provided steel beams for the first skyscraper in America, the Home Insurance Building in Chicago, Illinois. Homestead also produced steel used in the Washington Monument in Washington, D.C., and in elevated railroad tracks in Chicago and New York.

LOSS AND GAIN

As Carnegie reigned over the steel industry, he experienced big changes in his personal life. During the fall of 1886, Tom Carnegie fell ill with pneumonia. He died shortly thereafter. Carnegie, meanwhile, was battling a case of typhoid fever. Then, on November 10 of that same year, Margaret Carnegie died, also of pneumonia, at age 76. The death of his mother and brother affected Carnegie deeply. The family was very close; Carnegie had always lived with his mother. For a time after their deaths, he felt lost and lonely.

Loneliness turned to happiness, though, on April 22, 1887, when Carnegie married Louise Whitfield, a woman he

In July 1892, the workers at the Homestead Works went on strike, demanding higher wages. Carnegie was in Scotland at the time. He had left a man named Henry Clay Frick in charge. When workers went on strike, Carnegie's policy was to shut down the mill and wait for the workers to return. But when the Homestead workers struck, Frick shut down the mill and built a fence around it. He hired 300 security guards, called the Pinkertons, to keep out the striking workers. Violence soon broke out between the strikers and the security guards. By the time it was over, several people were dead and many others were injured. Eventually, the strike ended, and the mill reopened.

Carnegie's role in the Homestead strike has been debated for years. Most historians believe that had Carnegie been there, the violence might not have occurred. But Carnegie left Frick in charge of resolving the strike. Do you think Carnegie shares responsibility with Frick for what happened at the mill? Why?

had known for many years. She was the daughter of a successful New York merchant, and Carnegie met her through business dealings with her father. She was 21 years younger than Carnegie, who was 51 years old when they married. As part of their honeymoon, they visited Carnegie's hometown of Dunfermline. Louise loved Scotland so much that the couple rented a castle north of Dunfermline called Cluny Castle. The Carnegies visited the castle each year, inviting friends from Europe and America to join them.

After 10 years of marriage, the couple had their only child—a daughter they named Margaret, after Carnegie's mother. Though the Carnegies were extraordinarily wealthy, they didn't spoil Margaret. Instead, they taught her the importance of working hard and being responsible.

GIVING AWAY A FORTUNE

Carnegie believed that wealthy people should give away their money. He didn't think they should leave it to their children because this could spoil the children and leave them unwilling to earn their own money. He was also against leaving the money to other people and relying on them to give it to good causes. He feared that people might take the money for themselves. Carnegie believed that people who died with huge fortunes died in disgrace. He thought that wealthy people should give their money to colleges and universities, medical and scientific research, libraries, museums, and public parks—places that provide education and improve lives. Education, he said, was the key to ending problems such as poverty and unemployment.

*Louise and Andrew Carnegie had known one
another for several years before marrying.*

Back in 1881, Carnegie and his mother had returned to Dunfermline for what would be her final visit. The entire town, proud of Carnegie's success in America, turned out to greet them. Five bands played music. Dinners and cocktail parties were held in their honor. The most significant celebration occurred when Margaret laid the foundation stone for a library Carnegie was donating to the town. Even before paying for the library in Dunfermline, in 1869 Carnegie had paid for public baths to be built there. Carnegie's **philanthropy** soon spread far beyond his hometown.

In the mid-1880s, he donated money for disease research to a respected New York City hospital. And, despite his belief that money shouldn't be given directly to people in need, he was often seen handing out money to the poor, homeless, and hungry.

A library in Yorkville was the first branch of the New York Public Library to be built with funds from Carnegie.

In 1901, Carnegie sold his steel empire, which was by then called Carnegie Steel, to J. P. Morgan, a wealthy **financier**. The selling price was $380 million. Carnegie's share of the profits from the sale was $226 million. This brought his personal fortune to about $500 million. He was the richest man in the world.

After the sale of his empire, Carnegie began giving away his fortune. Because he believed that education was the key to a prosperous life, he donated a library to Allegheny City, his home when he first arrived in the United States. Carnegie then decided to build more libraries. He wanted his libraries to be free and open to anyone who wanted to use them. Any community that wanted a public library had to fill out a short application. The community had to promise to stock the library with books and to maintain it. As long as the community met these requirements, Carnegie approved the application. He funded hundreds of libraries around the country. Soon, communities around the world sought his money to build libraries. Carnegie responded, paying for libraries in Canada, Great Britain, South Africa, Australia, New Zealand, and elsewhere.

Carnegie also bought organs for Christian churches and Jewish synagogues. He had loved organ music since his boyhood. Although he wasn't religious, he respected people's religious beliefs. Carnegie supplied money to buy almost 8,000 organs in the United States, Canada, and Great Britain.

Carnegie supported several symphony orchestras, including one in Pittsburgh. He paid for the construction of New York City's Carnegie Hall, which opened in 1891. It is considered one of the finest concert halls in

the world. In Pittsburgh, Carnegie also donated an art gallery, a museum, and a concert hall. And he established a technical school in Pittsburgh that later became Carnegie-Mellon University.

In all, Carnegie gave money to about 400 colleges and universities. He also gave generously to trade schools and technical schools, which teach students specific skills such as welding, cooking, or office management. Most of his donations to colleges and other schools were meant to be used to build libraries, science laboratories, and similar buildings. In 1901, he gave $10 million to the four major universities in Scotland, which were in danger of closing because of a lack of money.

Though Carnegie enjoyed giving money to established institutions, he also liked starting new ones. In 1902, he gave $10 million to found the Carnegie Institution of Washington, D.C. Since its founding, the institution has supported many different projects, including scientific expeditions, exhibits, lectures, and educational materials.

After 10 years of giving away his fortune, Carnegie, now age 75, still had $180 million. So, in June 1911, he gave $25 million to set up the Carnegie Corporation, a foundation that would continue to

*In 1891, the opening of Carnegie Hall was
celebrated with a five-day festival.*

give away money in the future. He soon added another $100 million, and he also set up a foundation in Great Britain. Today, both foundations are still active.

By establishing the Carnegie Corporation and systematically giving away his money, Carnegie showed a new way for the wealthy to give away their fortunes. More importantly, he taught the wealthy that they had a responsibility to do good for others.

CHAPTER FIVE

A LIFE WELL LIVED

Skibo Castle is in the Northern Highlands of Scotland.

In his later years, Carnegie spent more time living in Scotland. He loved America, his adopted land, but his heart belonged to his homeland. In 1898, the year after his daughter, Margaret, was born, the Carnegies bought a Scottish estate named Skibo. Located on the coast of northern

Scotland, the estate covered 22,000 acres (8,900 hectares). It was surrounded by lakes, forests, streams, and trails for hiking and horseback riding. The Carnegies virtually rebuilt Skibo Castle, and they lived there for six months each year for the next 15 years.

One of Carnegie's greatest pleasures was telling young Margaret the same tales of Scottish heroes that his Uncle Lauder had told him. Though Carnegie traveled often during Margaret's childhood, he and his daughter exchanged many letters. Carnegie carried Margaret's letters in his wallet.

In 1901, the Carnegies built a grand mansion on the corner of Fifth Avenue and 91st Street in New York City. It had 64 rooms and six stories and was the first private home to have an elevator inside. Central Park was right across the street. Carnegie enjoyed brisk walks through the park. Sometimes he sat on a park bench and waited for strangers to sit down, too. He would strike up conversations with them, as if they were old friends. At home, Carnegie wrote letters and articles and oversaw the many causes he funded.

Shortly after World War I (1914–1918) broke out in Europe, the Carnegies returned from one of their extended stays at Skibo Castle. Though Carnegie didn't know it at the time, that would be his last trip to Scotland. The war prevented the Carnegies from returning to their beloved Scottish home, so they rented an estate in the Berkshire Hills of western Massachusetts. The estate, called Shadowbrook, included the second-largest private home in the United States. The area's blue lakes and green hills reminded the Carnegies of Scotland.

*The Carnegie Mansion in New York City is in an
area sometimes called Millionaires' Row.*

On April 22, 1919, the Carnegies celebrated their 32nd wedding
anniversary. On that same day, Margaret Carnegie married Roswell Miller,
a successful engineer. Both her parents gave her away at the ceremony.

Just months after Margaret's wedding, on August 11, 1919, Andrew Carnegie died of pneumonia at the Shadowbrook estate. He was 83 years old. When the world heard the news, hundreds of telegrams and letters—from family, friends, and world leaders—arrived at the estate. A few days later, Carnegie was buried at Sleepy Hollow Cemetery, near Tarrytown, New York. His gravestone is a cross made of granite from a **quarry** near Scotland's Skibo Castle with a simple inscription.

Carnegie's fortune at its height was believed to be about $500 million. This made him the richest man in the world. But by the time he died, he had given away most of it. As of June 1, 1918, a little more than a year before his death, Carnegie had given away more than 70 percent of his fortune. Upon his death, $25 million remained. True to his principles, he didn't leave money to Louise or Margaret. He had already provided for them financially. He did, however, leave all of his homes and property to Louise.

Of the remaining $25 million, Carnegie's will stated that $20 million go to the Carnegie Corporation. Carnegie also set aside $4 million as **pensions** for friends and others who had served him loyally over the years. These people included workers at the Skibo estate and the Carnegies' butler, housekeeper, nurse, and servants. The final $1 million was divided among several educational institutions. Carnegie had given away his entire fortune.

Today, Andrew Carnegie remains a well-known figure. His major foundations continue his charitable work. The Dunfermline cottage where he was born is now a museum dedicated to his life. His mansion on

In today's dollars, Carnegie would have been worth more than $100 billion. In contrast, Microsoft founder Bill Gates, the richest person in the world today, is worth about $50 billion. If you had $100 billion, how would you spend it?

Carnegie (seated, second from right) donated $600,000 to the Tuskegee Institute, a school in Alabama for African Americans that was founded by Booker T. Washington (seated, center).

Fifth Avenue in New York City is the world-famous Cooper-Hewitt, National Design Museum. Skibo Castle is a private club and luxury hotel, visited by rich and famous people from all over the world. And 3,000 Carnegie libraries still stand in the United States and around the world, encouraging and enhancing people's knowledge.

Andrew Carnegie is remembered as more than just a rich man who gave away a lot of money. He is considered the model for philanthropists everywhere. Before his death in 1996, David Packard, the cofounder of electronics giant Hewlett-Packard, gave away almost all of his $5 billion. He was called "today's Carnegie." And in 1997, an article in the journal *American Libraries* asked, "Is Bill Gates the New Andrew Carnegie?" Most of today's philanthropists are compared to Carnegie.

Andrew Carnegie was smart, charming, friendly, hardworking, and generous. He obtained great wealth but never forgot his poor start in Dunfermline. He believed that he had a responsibility to better the lives of others. Back in 1868, he wrote a memo to himself about retiring and devoting his life and fortune to good works. He fulfilled the goal he set for himself in that memo and became the most important figure in the history of philanthropy.

Carnegie once said, "Surplus wealth is a sacred trust, which its possessor is bound to administer in his lifetime for the good of the community."

TIMELINE

1800s America experiences rapid growth in size, transportation, industry, communication, and population.

1835 Andrew Carnegie is born on November 25, in Dunfermline, Scotland.

1840 Andrew's sister, Ann, is born, but she dies before her first birthday.

1843 Andrew's brother, Tom, is born; Andrew starts school; a steam-powered textile factory opens in Dunfermline, causing Andrew's father, William, to lose business.

1848 The Carnegie family leaves Scotland for America. They arrive in Allegheny City, Pennsylvania. Andrew goes to work in a cotton mill and a bobbin factory.

1850 Andrew begins work as a telegraph messenger.

1851 Andrew becomes a telegraph operator.

1853 Andrew Carnegie begins working for the Western Division of the Pennsylvania Railroad.

1855 Carnegie's father dies.

1858 Carnegie becomes a partner in the Woodruff Sleeping-Car Company.

1859 Carnegie is promoted to superintendent of the Western Division of the Pennsylvania Railroad; he also organizes the Columbia Oil Company.

1861 While the Civil War rages, Carnegie leads work crews repairing railroads and telegraph lines in the North.

1862 Carnegie organizes the Keystone Bridge Company.

1865 Carnegie quits the Pennsylvania Railroad to become a full-time investor. He founds the Superior Rail Mill, the Pittsburgh Locomotive Works, and the Union Iron Mills.

1867   Carnegie and his mother, Margaret, move to New York City.

1875   Carnegie's steel mill, the Edgar Thomson Steel Works, produces its first order of steel rails.

1881   Carnegie brings all his companies together and names the company Carnegie Brothers and Company; Carnegie and his mother visit Dunfermline and participate in the ceremonies for the construction of the first Carnegie library.

1883   Carnegie purchases the Homestead Works.

1886   Carnegie's mother and brother die.

1887   Carnegie marries Louise Whitfield on April 22.

1892   Carnegie Brothers and Company becomes Carnegie Steel Company; Carnegie is in Scotland during an important strike at the Homestead mill.

1897   Carnegie's daughter, Margaret, is born on March 30.

1901   Carnegie sells Carnegie Steel Company to J. P. Morgan for $380 million; Carnegie devotes himself to giving away his fortune.

1911   Carnegie establishes the Carnegie Corporation.

1914–1918   World War I is fought in Europe, preventing Carnegie from returning to Scotland.

1919   Carnegie's daughter, Margaret, marries on April 22; Carnegie dies on August 11 and is buried near Tarrytown, New York.

GLOSSARY

apprentices (uh-PREN-tis-sez) people who learn a trade or craft by working with a skilled person

buggy (BUHG-ee) a light carriage with two wheels pulled by a horse

entrepreneur (ON-truh-pruh-NUR) someone who organizes, manages, and takes on the risks of a business

financier (fuh-nan-SIR) a person who deals with finance and investment on a large scale

innovation (in-uh-VAY-shuhn) a new idea or invention

invaluable (in-VAL-yuh-buhl) very useful or precious

investor (in-VEST-er) a person who gives or lends money to something, such as a company, in the belief that he or she will get more money back in the future

molten (MOHL-tuhn) melted by intense heat

motivated (MOH-tuh-vay-ted) provided with a reason, such as a need or desire, to act

opportunity (op-ur-TOO-nuh-tee) a good chance for advancement or progress

pensions (PEN-shuhnz) fixed amounts of money paid regularly to people who have retired from work

philanthropy (fuh-LAN-thruh-pee) helping others by giving time or money to causes and charities

prosperous (PROSS-pur-uhss) successful or thriving

quarry (KWOR-ee) a place where stone, slate, or minerals are dug from the ground

textile (TEK-steyel) a fabric or cloth that has been woven or knitted

treason (TREE-zuhn) the crime of attempting to overthrow the government of your country; betraying your country by helping an enemy during a war or by spying for another country

FOR MORE INFORMATION

Books

Edge, Laura Bufano. *Andrew Carnegie: Industrial Philanthropist.* Minneapolis, MN: Lerner Publishing Group, 2003.

Halpern, Monica. *Railroad Fever: Building the Transcontinental Railroad.* Hanover, PA: National Geographic Children's Books, 2004.

Levy, Patricia. *Scotland.* Tarrytown, NY: Marshall Cavendish, 2000.

Pierce, Alan. *The Industrial Revolution.* Edina, MN: ABDO Publishing Group, 2005.

Web Sites

America's Story from America's Library: Andrew Carnegie
www.americaslibrary.gov/cgi-bin/page.cgi/aa/carnegie
Includes photos and a timeline of Carnegie's life that parallels the same time in U.S. history.

Carnegie Corporation of New York: Carnegie for Kids
www.carnegie.org/sub/kids/index.html
Features information about the founding of the Carnegie
Corporation as well as a timeline and images

Carnegie Museums of Pittsburgh
www.carnegiemuseums.org
Offers many interactive exhibits

INDEX

ABOUT THE AUTHOR

Sarah De Capua is the author of many books, including biographies and historical titles. She was born and raised in Connecticut. She currently lives in Colorado, where she often borrows books from her community's Carnegie library, which was built in 1904.